LARRY THE FRILLED-NECK LIZARD

LARRY THE FRILLED-NECK LIZARD

In Association with:
Elite Online Publishing
63 East 11400 South
Suite #230
Sandy, UT 84070
EliteOnlinePublishing.com

ISBN: 979-8376271148 (Paperback)
ISBN: 978-1513677071 (Hardback)

LARRY THE
FRILLED-NECK LIZARD

JENNY SCHREIBER

MEET LARRY THE
FRILLED-NECK LIZARD,
HE IS ALSO KNOWN AS
THE FRILLED DRAGON.

WHEN LARRY IS SCARED
OR ANGRY, THE LARGE
FRILL AROUND HIS NECK
OPENS UP TO MAKE
HIMSELF LOOK BIGGER.

HE IS AN AGAMID
LIZARD, WHICH MEANS
HE HAS A SPECIAL
HINGE IN HIS JAW THAT
ALLOWS HIM TO OPEN
HIS MOUTH VERY WIDE.

THE FRILLED-NECK
LIZARD USES GREEN OR
BROWN COLOR TO
CAMOUFLAGE HIMSELF
TO BLEND IN WITH HIS
SURROUNDINGS.

LARRY CAN CHANGE
COLORS BASED ON THE
TEMPERATURE AND
HUMIDITY.

LARRY IS AN EXCELLENT CLIMBER, AND CAN BE FOUND IN TREES AND BUSHES.

HE CAN RUN ON HIS
HIND LEGS LIKE A
DINOSAUR!

HE CAN RUN ON HIS
HIND LEGS LIKE A
DINOSAUR!

LARRY IS A PREDATOR
WHO USES A SURPRISE
ATTACK TO EAT INSECTS,
SPIDERS, AND SMALL
REPTILES.

LARRY CAN GROW UP TO
1 METER LONG, WHICH IS
ABOUT
39 INCHES
OR 3 FEET.

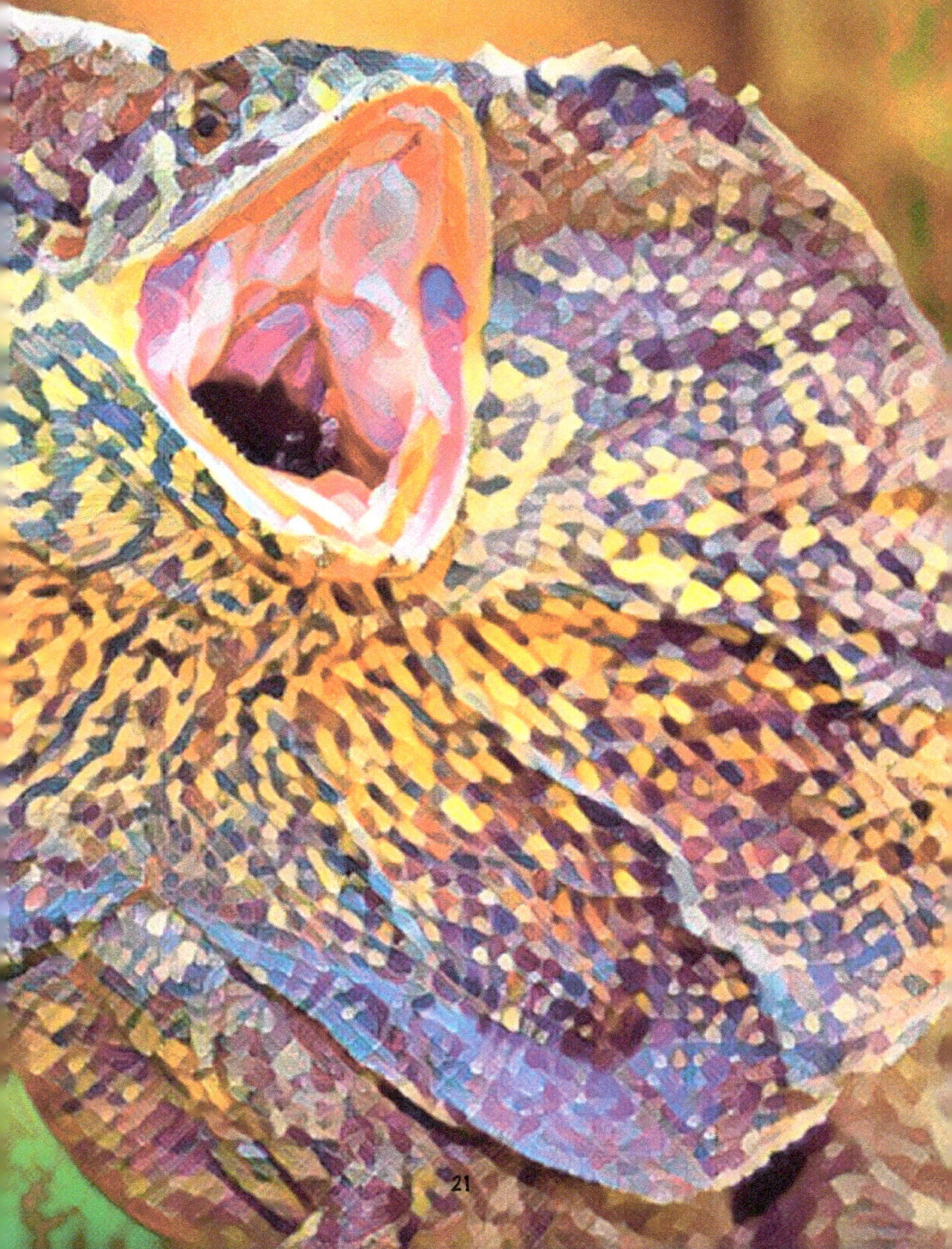

LARRY THE
THE FRILLED-NECK
LIZARD CAN LIVE UP TO
15 YEARS IN
THE WILD.

LARRY IS ACTIVE
DURING THE DAY AND
RESTS AT NIGHT.

LARRY IS FOUND IN
THE WILD,
IN AUSTRALIA AND IN
SOUTHERN
NEW GUINEA.

LARRY'S FEMALE
FRIENDS LAY EGGS IN
THE WILD, USUALLY IN
THE SUMMER.

LARRY'S FEMALE
FRIENDS LAY EGGS IN
THE WILD, USUALLY IN
THE SUMMER.

LARRY IS TERRITORIAL
AND WILL DEFEND HIS
HABITAT FROM
OTHER MALES.

LARRY LIKES TO BE
ALONE AND ONLY COMES
TOGETHER WITH OTHERS
DURING THE MATING
SEASON.

33

LARRY IS NOT
DANGEROUS TO HUMANS
AND HE IS A SHY LIZARD.

33

LARRY IS NOT
DANGEROUS TO HUMANS
AND HE IS A SHY LIZARD.

THE FRILLED-NECK
LIZARD IS A PROTECTED
SPECIES.

THE END

THE FRILLED-NECK LIZARD IS A UNIQUE AND FASCINATING ANIMAL THAT IS FUN TO WATCH IN THE WILD.

Find More books by Jenny Schreiber

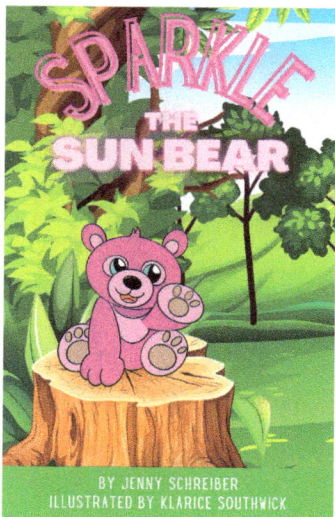

Sparkle the Sun Bear

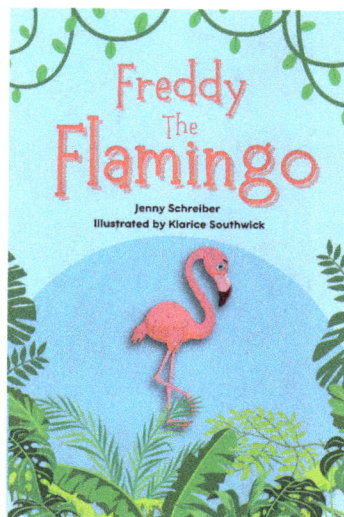

Freddy the Flamingo

Piper the
Polar Bear

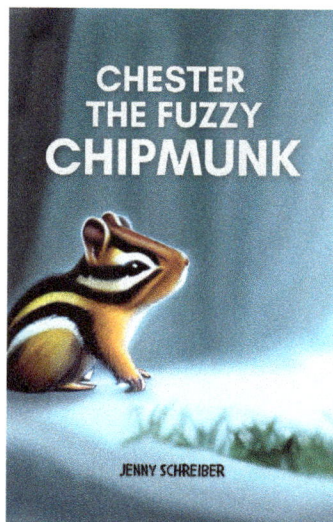

Chester the
Fuzzy Chipmunk

Animal Facts Children's Book Series

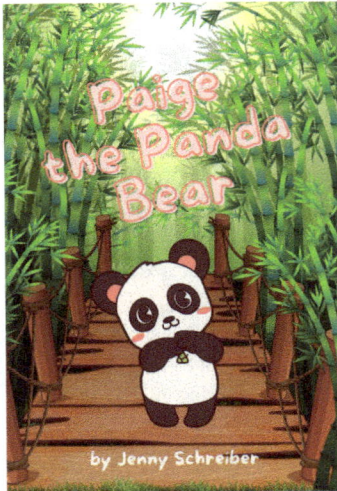

Paige the
Panda Bear

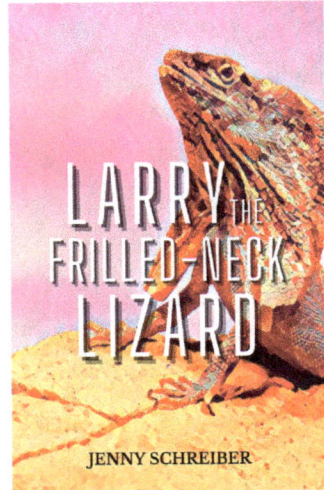

Larry the
Frilled-Neck Lizard

www.ingramcontent.com/pod-product-compliance
Lightning Source LLC
Chambersburg PA
CBHW071823050426
42335CB00063BA/1785